The Way of the Passion

The Way of the Passion

FORTY STATIONS WITH JESUS

Julien Chilcott-Monk

BOOKS & MEDIA
Boston

Library of Congress Cataloging-in-Publication Data

Chilcott-Monk, J. P.
  The way of the Passion : forty stations with Jesus / Julien
Chilcott-Monk.
     pages cm
  ISBN 978-0-8198-8348-3 -- ISBN 0-8198-8348-4
  1. Jesus Christ--Passion--Prayers and devotions. 2. Stations of the
Cross--Prayers and devotions. 3. Lent--Prayers and devotions. 4.
Passion narratives (Gospels)--Prayers and devotions. 5. Catholic
Church--Prayers and devotions. I. Title.
  BT431.3.C49 2015
  232.96--dc23

                    201401618

Scripture quotations from the *Revised Standard Version of the Bible*, copyright © 1952 [2nd edition, 1971] by the Division of Christian Education of the National Council of the Churches of Christ in the United States of America. Used by permission. All rights reserved.

Cover design by Rosana Usselmann

Cover art: Stefano Maria Legnani

"P" and PAULINE are registered trademarks of the Daughters of Saint Paul.

Published by Pauline Books & Media, 50 Saint Pauls Avenue, Boston, MA 02130-3491

Printed in the U.S.A.

www.pauline.org

Pauline Books & Media is the publishing house of the Daughters of Saint Paul, an international congregation of women religious serving the Church with the communications media.

1 2 3 4 5 6 7 8 9   19 18 17 16 15

To TSRH

Contents

Introduction

This Lenten companion is intended to ignite ideas and fresh thoughts about forty episodes of the passion of our Lord. It offers a "station" every day throughout Lent—Sundays are omitted, of course—from Ash Wednesday to Holy Saturday. The non-canonical material contained here is the result of the author's "reading between the lines" of the Gospel narratives and is meant to help the pilgrim focus more clearly on the events we recall ceremonially during Holy Week.

The Gospels give us only the essential details of the passion because a meticulous report of the proceedings is not the intention of the evangelists, who are concerned primarily with our Lord's teaching and in establishing, in the light of the resurrection, who he is and how he fulfills God's promise of a Savior. However, 2,000 years later we find it helpful to enter more fully into these events in order to feel something of the horror and trauma experienced by Jesus and those around him, and so grasp more easily the impact of his teaching and how our salvation was secured.

In reflecting on these daily episodes, the pilgrim can explore fresh and personal paths of contemplation by giving his or her mind free rein throughout the forty days.

To complete each session, a prompt or two is given to aid further self-examination or intercession before the more formal suggested prayers. An expanded *Paternoster* is given in the Appendix as an aid to fuller intercession.

The translation of the Holy Bible used in this book is the Catholic Edition of the *Revised Standard Version*, which, in the author's view, is still the best. In the text, quotations from the RSV are given in italics, but transliterations, conjectural speech, and the author's translations are given in Roman type.

The present tense is frequently employed in this book to give immediacy to the narrative.

JULIEN CHILCOTT-MONK
(Saint Veronica's Day)

STATION 1

The Entry into Jerusalem

Most of the crowd spread their garments on the road, and others cut branches from the trees and spread them on the road (Matthew 21:8).

Jesus intended to ride on a donkey; his instructions were specific. He would ride into Jerusalem on the traditional mount of a monarch who rides to his people in peace.

The twelve disciples are now keeping pace beside the donkey. It is of no discomfort to them. They are content because the crowds are gathering. It is exciting. At last, the Master is properly acclaimed as he rides toward the capital. No need for all those predictions of gloom and suffering after all. Why, people are spreading tokens of allegiance as if before a king. Someone is crying out, *"Hosanna to the Son of David!"* (This person must know a thing or two, because King David reconciled his people by choosing Jerusalem as a neutral capital.) However, at the moment, Jesus is riding happily with his band of students. He is bantering with the crowds, always good for a joke and witty repartee. He acknowledges friends and acquaintances in the swelling body of enthusiasm. (But does he see among them the agents of Annas and Caiaphas, in little knots of dissent?)

Jesus enters the city, honored and greeted with fronds, in deep contrast to the manner in which he will shortly leave the city—through the northwestern gate and on to the hill of Golgotha.

By means of this ride into Jerusalem our Lord is perhaps declaring: "Here gathered around me are my disciples. For three years I have been preparing them with the words you have heard me preach. I bring them with me into the city from which they will emerge as my body and my Church. They are here for their final lesson and examination. This is the meaning of my journey. I come to claim my crown, but it will be a crown of sorrow and of thorns, because that is the only way in which I can lead my subjects to the kingdom of heaven. And so, take me in place of all humanity. Take me instead of accusing them, because I shall carry their sin with me."

And so the king comes to claim his crown. This journey of resolution takes Jesus to the climax of his ministry; his disciples are ready to face their trials and tests of faith. (We have knowledge of the risen Christ; at this stage, the disciples do not. We have the benefit of the Church's teaching about these final events; at this stage, the disciples do not.) And the crown Jesus claims is, of course, the crown of thorns.

Let us consider the change in people's hearts that transforms their "Hosanna!" of adulation into their "Crucify!" of hate.

O Heavenly Father, whose Son rode in triumph to the city of Jerusalem, mercifully assist us to understand fully the triumph of the cross and the goal of our hope in relation to the power and pleasures of our earthly desires.

Our Father . . . Hail Mary . . . Glory be . . .

STATION 2

The Anointing of Jesus at Bethany

Jesus came to Bethany. . . . There they made him a supper . . . (John 12:1–8).

John's Gospel tells us that the anointing of Jesus takes place shortly before the entry into Jerusalem, but Matthew and Mark suggest otherwise. Only John identifies the woman with the precious ointment as Mary, the sister of Martha, whom we meet earlier in the ministry of Jesus in Luke's Gospel. There we find Mary content to sit beside Jesus while her sister busies herself with the food preparation. Martha complains to our Lord, who reassures her about the different roles people are chosen to play. Here the scene is similar: Jesus is resting at the house in Bethany, not far from Jerusalem. As before, Martha prepares and serves the food. Perhaps we can place ourselves within this scene, standing there in the light and knowledge of the resurrection. Martha sighs at the sight of her sister lazing at the feet of Jesus, hanging on his every word. On this occasion, however, she does not comment.

One of the great treasures of the household is the expensive oil extracted from the roots and stems of the Indian flower, *spikenard*. Its sublime fragrance; its many medicinal properties; its effect as an essential oil for the well-being of limbs and muscles—all contribute to its reputation and value. It is always used most sparingly and sometimes is not used at all, simply kept as an investment. But without any inhibitions or caution, Mary opens the box and applies the contents generously to our Lord's feet. Are we shocked at the waste? Judas certainly seems to be, but his motives are not necessarily honorable. *"Let her alone,"* Jesus exclaims to Judas. *"Let her keep it for the day of my burial."* He then adds the telling phrase, *"The poor are always with you,"* knowing, as he does, the reputation Judas has of borrowing from the poor box.

The house is now *"filled with the fragrance of the ointment"* as Mary massages our Lord's feet and wipes away the excess oil with her hair. In doing so she repairs the wear and tear of recent journeys and anticipates the more devastating damage to come—the bruising from his stumbles along the *Via Dolorosa* and the penetration of the nails. Her ministry also anticipates Jesus's burial, as the oil represents those other costly spices prepared for the tomb but never properly applied; it represents our constant duty to the poor and the less fortunate, who are ever present often because of our neglect. This anticipation of our

Lord's passion leads us to consider the moment when Jesus will pray to the Father for the forgiveness of our sins—past, present, and future—which are blotted out with his sacrifice.

Why are the poor always with us? Is it simply because of our neglect? Does the knowledge that our sins of neglect have already been forgiven affect in any way the level of our generosity to the poor this Lent?

O Lord, whose companions on earth were often sinful men and women, grant us strength to react to the promptings of the Holy Spirit and acknowledge the sins of which we are guilty.

Our Father . . . Hail Mary . . . Glory be . . .

STATION 3

Preparation for the Passover

Go and prepare the Passover for us . . . and they pre-pared the Passover (Luke 22:7–13).

We picture the scene. The Passover is nearly upon them and the disciples seek instructions from the Lord (Mt 26:17–19). They know that their little fraternity will celebrate the feast with Jesus in the traditional way. He gives them directions to the place he has previously chosen. But Luke's account provides us with a little more detail. The directions are precise and are given to Peter and John, who are instructed to make the necessary preparations. They are entering the final chapter, for it is at this special meal that Jesus will institute the Holy Eucharist, which will sustain Holy Church into the future. The detail of the preparation, therefore, is important.

The disciples are instructed to *"go into the city."* Where are they? Perhaps they are in the Temple precinct or at the foot of the Mount of Olives where they were lodging.

They go into the lower city and across to the southwestern corner. As instructed, they follow a water-carrier on his way to deliver water to the house in question. As we watch the two disciples we are reminded (as we are when we touch the water in the holy water font) of the need for proper preparation. We have the advantage over the two disciples. We know that soon our Lord will wash their feet with this very water and teach them the profound lessons about purification and service to others. We meet the owner of the house, who is not surprised at the question *"Where is the Master to eat the Passover with his disciples?"* He seems proud to show us the upper room of his shop and dwelling, accessible only by means of an exterior, wooden stairway. The room is made ready with palm-leaf matting around a long, low table, so that the meal can be enjoyed in the modern manner. Peter and John provide additional refinements and adjust the matting. They have followed our Lord's instructions with precision.

❧◈❧

The disciples did not question our Lord; they obeyed his directions to the letter. When we prepare for an event, the detail is often crucial, but preparation always has the ultimate goal and destination in mind and in view. When we prepare for Mass, for example, it is on the Mass that we focus.

Give us the self-control that springs
From discipline of outward things,
That fasting inward secretly
The soul may purely dwell with thee.

> — *Attributed to Saint Gregory the Great,*
> *"Audi, benign Conditor"*

Father in heaven, forgive us our daily omissions and assist us in our desire to live a holy Lent in order to prepare for the celebration of your Son's glorious resurrection.

Our Father . . . Hail Mary . . . Glory be . . .

STATION 4

Jesus Washes the Feet of His Disciples

Then he poured water into a basin, and began to wash the disciples' feet, and to wipe them with the towel with which he was girded (John 13:5).

Provision of water for the washing of feet was the mark of an attentive and hospitable host. After all, sandals and sandy soil meant that water for the feet was always welcome, even after a short journey. Indeed, the disciples probably had already washed their feet on arrival, when they kicked off their footwear at the top of the outside stairway.

How do we visualize the scene? Perhaps a towel is draped over a three-legged stool in the corner of the room, along with an earthenware jug and bowl. The Beloved Disciple is positioned to the right of the place just vacated by Jesus; Judas is on the left. Are we among the disciples? Perhaps we are to the right of Simon Peter, who is wondering what to say because he has been fidgeting in that characteristic way of his. And when our Lord arrives beside him, Peter declares: *"You shall never wash my feet"*; you are not going to humiliate yourself for me! *"If I do not wash you,"* Jesus replies,*"you have no part in me."* Peter thinks quickly: *"Lord, not my feet only, but also my hands and my head!"* (Jn 13:8–10) *Only Peter*, we think as we await our turn, *big blustering fisherman that he is*. Jesus replies gently: "What I am doing is sufficient, and the point of the exercise will be made apparent." We feel for Peter because he often articulates the daft responses that we might have made. Jesus comes to us and we are silent. *"Do you know what I have done to you?"* The message slowly dawns upon us, perhaps not immediately but sometime later. We see Jesus at Golgotha as the naked man bending before us, and in him we see the Heavenly Father condescending to humanity, suffering with the burden of humanity's rejection of God. We are reminded of our freedom from original sin through the baptismal waters, but we know that if we are to have part with Christ, we must be prepared to enter with him into his passion and death.

⚜

"Do you know what I have done to you?" Do we grasp the instruction? It is certainly not limited to washing the feet of our friends, to cleaning their shoes, to being hospitable. The lesson of this acted parable is much more profound. As the Creator cares for the needs of his creatures, so must

we care for the needs of others. The vocation of serving others, of being *other Christs*, is our general Christian vocation, to be exercised along with the vocation that is specific to us.

O Heavenly Father, who condescended to humanity, may the way we live our lives always reflect your Son's example of service to others.

Our Father . . . Hail Mary . . . Glory be . . .

STATION 5

The Warning of Betrayal

"Truly, I say to you, one of you will betray me."
"Is it I, Lord?" (Matthew 26:20, 22)

"Truly, truly, I say to you, one of you will betray me."
"Lord, who is it?" (John 13:21–30)

Jesus was always conscious of discontent, and he was acutely aware of any murmurings of dissent. He knew what was in the hearts of those around him; he read Judas clearly. Of course Jesus was aware of the rumors circulating among the disciples that Judas was dipping into the common purse for his own purposes. It is likely that Jesus knew Judas might be susceptible to silver in exchange for false witness. He knew that his mission would culminate in horror; that the Heavenly Father's will was that the Son of Man would first have to suffer in order to redeem.

We have already visited the upper room. We know how they lounge on the floor beside the low table. Leaning on their left elbows and forearms, they eat with their right hands. For moments of ritual, a more formal posture is adopted, and the men rise and sit back on their heels. Our Lord is alongside Judas Iscariot; John, whom we identify as the Beloved Disciple, is next to our Lord; and Peter lounges beside John. The confidential enquiry Peter makes of John, *"Tell us, who it is of whom he speaks,"* can be whispered easily and passed from John to Jesus: *"Lord, who is it?"* Jesus points to the traitor in a rather enigmatic way. At this stage only John knows the significance of the dipped bread. On such an occasion it would not have been an extraordinary act, but in the light of what Jesus says, this sign seems to confirm the commission Judas has already accepted. *"Then . . . Satan entered into him."* Satan is he who obstructs, who comes between us and God as an almost impenetrable barrier; in a sense, we give him life and flesh. Satan will blind Judas as to the right course of action until it is too late. The morsel of bread is probably dipped in a confection of ground almonds and chopped apricots, a pleasant complement to the bitter herbs. He leaves the room with the words ringing in his ears: *"What you are going to do, do quickly."*

ꙮ

Satan obstructs. Satan steps between us and God, between us and our Christian duty. Satan is the idol we eagerly put before us in place of God, the idol that comes in the guise of all the attractive things that persuade us away from our love of God. In indulging ourselves we indulge Satan and give him flesh and blood. As with Adam, we always begin with the sin of pride.

Therefore behold thy Church, O Lord,
And grace of penitence accord
To all who seek with generous tears
Renewal of their wasted years.

— Anonymous, "Jesu, quadragenariae"
(ninth century)

Our Father . . . Hail Mary . . . Glory be . . .

STATION 6

The Institution of the Eucharist

"Take, eat: this is my body" (Matthew 26:26–29).

The words of the institution of the Eucharist are well known to us, but perhaps we can benefit from spending a moment or two at that table prepared by Peter and John. John records, after the departure of Judas Iscariot, how all was made clear to the remaining disciples, so much so that they acknowledge: *"Ah, now you are speaking plainly, not in any figure!"* (Jn 16:29). It is Philip, however, who elicits these words from our Lord: *"He who has seen me has seen the Father"* and *"Believe me, that I am in the Father and the Father in me"* (Jn 14:9, 11). Secure in this knowledge, the disciples are ready for their final lesson before the horror of the final hours begins. We lounge beside the table opposite Jesus. The disciples have already heard, some time ago, these words from their Master's lips, *"I am the bread of life. . . . I am the living bread which came down from heaven"* (Jn 6:48–51). They stayed with him even though they did not understand. Now he puts all these sayings into perspective and completes the picture. And what he next does and says give rise to no query or comment from the disciples. We do not detect any astonishment.

Now as they were eating, Jesus took bread, blessed and broke it, and gave it to the disciples and said,

"Take, eat; this is my body." And he took a cup, and when he had given thanks he gave it to them, saying, "Drink of it, all of you; for this is my blood of the covenant, which is poured out for many for the forgiveness of sins" (Mt 26:26–28).

This is a night of contrasts. The disciples have been taught the lesson of service; they know one of them is seeking to betray Jesus; they now know unequivocally that the Heavenly Father and their Master are one. Everything is in place for their complete understanding, when they consider this night afresh in the light of the resurrection.

What a glorious gift is the gift of the Holy Eucharist. Not only does Jesus give life to the Church, but he gives the Church his Body as food. He is as present in the Blessed Sacrament as he was in the manger at Bethlehem.

Let us never underestimate or treat this gift casually.

At the last great Supper lying
Circled by his brethren's band,

Meekly with the law complying,
First he finished his command,
Then, immortal food supplying,
Gave himself with his own hand.

> — *Saint Thomas Aquinas, "Pange, lingua gloriosi*
> *Corporis mysterium"*

Our Father . . . Hail Mary . . . Glory be . . .

STATION 7   *Jesus Predicts Peter's Denials*

"Simon, Simon, behold, Satan demanded to have you. . . . I tell you, Peter, the cock will not crow this day, until you three times deny that you know me" (Luke 22:31–34).

Let us not be complacent about our resistance to Satan. Peter was ever confident in all matters. But our Lord knew well how often this bluff, assertive character had blundered and had said and done the wrong thing, always with the best intentions. Jesus would say to him: "Stop, think, listen. Consider things carefully." The other disciples must have been grateful to Peter for his outspokenness, for asking the questions they might have asked, for making the absurd statements they might have made. Why did our Lord nickname him *Peter*? Was there ever anyone less like a rock? But that is what Jesus was training him to be. How unlikely! Nevertheless, let us never suppose that we cannot be changed and molded by Christ if we allow him to do so.

Peter's nerve will fail at the crucial hour, when confronted by the fear of arrest and condemnation by his association with Jesus. As we have been present with the disciples ever since the magnificent entry into Jerusalem, we experience the shock felt by the others, and, of course, by Peter himself, when our Lord predicts Peter's three denials. How crestfallen he must feel when Jesus says, *"Simon, Satan demanded to have you."* And then Jesus goes on to confirm Peter in his role as leader of the Church by continuing: *"When you have turned again, strengthen your brethren."* Jesus looks beyond our sin toward the fulfillment of our potential and our vocation. But Peter does not know when to stop: *"Lord, I am ready to go with you to prison and to death."* He is clearly not ready yet. *"I tell you, Peter, the cock will not crow this day until you three times deny that you know me."* Peter is devastated.

***

Our Lord overlooks our sins and weaknesses, the sins we are yet to commit. Remember, he has already forgiven us. He can see our potential, our ability to fulfill the vocation given to us. His sacrifice makes all sin forgivable and forgiven, and the waters of Baptism wash away the guilt of inherited sin, the memory of the sin of Adam. But we still need to penitently ask Jesus for forgiveness.

Thy grace have we offended sore,
By sins, O God, which we deplore;
But pour upon us from on high,
O pardoning One, thy clemency.

> — *Attributed to Saint Gregory the Great,*
> *"Ex more docti mystico"*

Our Father . . . Hail Mary . . . Glory be . . .

STATION 8   *Jesus in Gethsemane*

And they went to a place which was called Gethsemane;
and he said to his disciples, "Sit here, while I pray"
(Mark 14:32).

And so we walk across the lower city and out to the
foot of the Mount of Olives to the place of the olive
press. Here the disciples would often meet to talk, dis-
cuss, and pray. Jesus would teach them and prepare them
for the time to come.

On this night Jesus needs to be alone but, nevertheless, to know that his friends are near. Those closest to
him hear his impassioned plea to the Heavenly Father. He
knows the time is drawing near when he will be taken; he
knows precisely what his mission is. However, at this crucial point he needs to confirm the Father's will and, at the
same time, make clear that he and the Father are of the
same mind. Jesus has to show his disciples that he is
wholly committed to the will of the Father. This is no

simple matter, for in his humanity the prospect is daunting; even so, Jesus, in his agony, accepts without question the will of the Father. The feeling of terror having subsided, Jesus is left temporarily in a weakened state. In a foretaste of his final passion here in Gethsemane, among the olives and olive presses where oil is squeezed from the fruit—the oil that sustains, preserves, and anoints the sick, the feeble, and kings—he sweats blood for us.

Let us picture Gethsemane with its olive presses—some in good order, others broken. The trees are regimented, well-tended, and healthy. The area around the presses has, over the years, been bathed in spilt oil. The disciples close to Jesus overhear his prayers. They experience the agony and the chilling terror Jesus feels in his humanity. He has to bring before his Heavenly Father his life's work; he has to ensure that his will and that of his Father are one and that they are of the same mind. Having established that, he is strengthened. Any lingering doubts and uncertainties about his commission are dispelled. The disciples see him gradually recover his composure, comforted by the unseen angel of his holy Father. His necessary crisis over, he falls into contemplation, and his disciples fall asleep.

Jesus kneels—maybe with his forehead on the ground. The sweat has now gone and his face is anointed with the spilt oil ready for his coronation.

And in the garden secretly,
And on the cross on high,
Should teach His brethren and inspire
To suffer and to die.

— *Blessed J. H. Newman, "The Dream of Gerontius"*

Our Father . . . Hail Mary . . . Glory be . . .

STATION 9

Jesus Is Arrested

Then they came up and laid hands on Jesus and seized him (Matthew 26:50).

Suddenly a disturbance takes place, followed by a great commotion. Are we still among the startled disciples or are we now with the swaggering mob? Judas has done his work admirably: he knows the favorite places and where an arrest can be made discreetly. After all, Jesus has many friends and other disciples in the city. There will be plenty of time in the morning for the temple officials to work on the crowd, stirring up hatred and a change of heart among his followers, and anger among the indifferent. How easy it is with a small band of armed men and, of course, the elders of the people to give the enterprise among the olive trees the authority it needs.

Judas has told the gang that, on arrival at Gethsemane, he will formally identify Jesus as the perpetrator of the reported crimes with a kiss of friendship. No argument can be made to suggest that the arrest is anything but completely legitimate. He is identified by a witness, after all, albeit a false witness.

There is a skirmish and a blade flashes. *"And behold, one of those who were with Jesus stretched out his hand and drew his sword, and struck the slave of the high priest, and cut off his ear"* (Mt 26:51). Perhaps at this stage Judas is concerned that the arrest is not the easy matter he guaranteed to the chief priests. "No more of this," Jesus commands. *"Put your sword back into its place; for all who take the sword will perish by the sword"* (Mt 26:52). For the moment, Jesus's authority is accepted by both sides, although he is about to be taken into custody. Perhaps among the arresting gang there is palpable fear of what they have taken on. Perhaps Judas is harboring doubts about the chain of events he has set in motion. But it is all too late. The gang is large enough to subdue the disciples, who put up no further resistance. Indeed, they are in fear for their own freedom. *"Then all the disciples forsook him and fled"* (Mt 26:56).

⚜

How often do we forsake him? How often have we, as Christians, set Christ up for a fall by our un-Christian behavior? The Church, in the eyes of the world, is only what is seen in us.

O Heavenly Father, give us the strength to resist any inclination we may have to do the work of Satan, to injure the Church and to diminish her reputation in the eyes of the world.

Our Father . . . Hail Mary . . . Glory be . . .

Jesus Is Taken Before Annas

First they led him to Annas; for he was the father-in-law of Caiaphas, who was high priest that year. "I have said nothing secretly. Why do you ask me? Ask those who have heard me, what I said to them; they know what I said" (John 18:13–24).

John and Peter have followed Jesus at a safe distance after running away at Gethsemane. They can now do nothing more than watch and wait.

Taking Jesus to Annas may well have been intended to unsettle Jesus before proceeding to the High Priest. Indeed, the violence begins almost immediately. Jesus is questioned about his teaching and points out the absurdity of the question, since daily the chief priests have witnessed and heard his preaching and teaching. There has been nothing clandestine, nothing secret. His utterances have always been made to the widest possible public. Jesus deals with the questions in a masterful manner and succinctly points out that his accusers lack evidence of anything improper and therefore have no case against him. He is slapped in the face. *"Is that how you answer the high priest?"* Jesus then suggests that striking him will not necessarily improve their case.

We surmise that John himself witnessed these exchanges and saw the Master moved on to Caiaphas, who had been nominated that year to reside in the High Priest's official quarters.

Do we intervene and declare Jesus innocent and give an account of the nature and meaning of our Lord's teaching? Do we tell the authorities that Jesus is there to fulfill and not abolish the Law? No, we actually remain silent and make no offer of ourselves as witnesses for the defense.

⚜

Do we even now keep our Christianity and Catholicism for Sundays?

Father in heaven, whose Son was treated with disdain in the court Annas convened to intimidate, grant us the confidence and the words to speak when we ought to speak.

Remember thou, though frail we be,
That yet thine handiwork are we;

Nor let the honour of thy name
Be by another put to shame.

> — *Attributed to Saint Gregory the Great,*
> *"Ex more docti mystico"*

Our Father . . . Hail Mary . . . Glory be . . .

STATION 11 *Peter's First Denial*

Then a maid, seeing him as he sat in the light and gazing at him, said, "This man also was with him" (Luke 22:56).

Peter is spoken to by one of the maids of the high priest. Nervous and jumpy, Peter is in the courtyard waiting for news of the Lord. John has left him in order to find out more about Jesus's fate. Our Lord's prediction lurks in the back of Peter's mind. He still does not believe that he will be so weak and spineless. However, he is worried.

A fire kindles in the center of the courtyard, and servants and officers of the high priests Annas and Caiaphas are warming themselves. Peter is among them, trying to remain incognito. He wonders whether he ought to leave and seek safety elsewhere. He naturally feels uncomfortable in the company of our Lord's enemies. A confusion of bravery and stubbornness keeps him there. Yes, he'll stay and show the other disciples that Jesus was only pulling his leg when he made the prediction—the Master's way of helping Peter to focus his mind on what was unfolding hour by hour. He'll remain in the courtyard listening to the general banter, keeping warm by the fire. He'll stand his ground.

As he is enjoying the warmth and watching the sparks fly heavenward, a servant-girl, who has been looking at Peter rather carefully, says: *"This man also was with him."* According to Luke, she says this to a companion or to the general company rather than to Peter, but he, through his own sense of self-preservation, awakens out of his reverie and gives an instant and angry rebuttal: *"Woman, I do not know him!"* Somewhat satisfied, she changes the subject and begins talking to her companion. Peter is left wallowing in self-pity or in the agony of knowing that he has already begun to betray Jesus as surely as Judas has done.

⁂

Not speaking for someone when we have the opportunity, as we have seen, is a bedfellow with calumny, detraction, and false witness. Peter must have agonized over the question: Why did I not concentrate on the commission the Master had given me? *"When you have turned again, look after your brethren."*

We all have our Peter moments and we remember them with shame. We can daily deny Christ in our own personal ways, almost without thinking. Happily our Lord looks beyond what he knows will be a stumbling block for us and says: *"When you have turned . . ."*

Our hearts are open, Lord, to thee:
Thou knowest our infirmity;
Pour out on all who seek thy face
Abundance of thy pardoning grace.

> — *Attributed to Saint Gregory the Great,*
> *"Audi, benign Conditor"*

Our Father . . . Hail Mary . . . Glory be . . .

STATION 12

Jesus Before Caiaphas, and Peter's Further Denials

Annas then sent him bound to Caiaphas, the high priest (John 18:24).

But Peter said, "Man, I do not know what you are saying." And immediately while he was still speaking, the cock crowed (Luke 22:60).

Annas then passes Jesus over to be questioned under the jurisdiction of his son-in-law, Caiaphas, the high priest that year.

While in the care of Caiaphas and, presumably, in full view of the bystanders warming themselves, the guards begin to have sport with this prisoner. They blindfold him and jeer; they swivel him around and slap him over the head. They laugh the laugh of the bully; the confident laugh of the man with power over another; the laugh of the untouchable. *"Prophesy!"* they cry with playground glee, *"Who is it that struck you?"* (Lk 22:64). Perhaps they eventually become bored with the short-lived pleasure of taunting this prisoner—after all, they cannot get him to cower and beg.

As Peter nurses his bruised ego, Jesus, his blindfold now removed, is shackled to a post. Can Peter already see the effects of the beating suffered by Jesus? The memory of the maid's observation and his response has subsided, and Peter begins to feel wretched at Jesus's plight. Then someone suddenly agrees with the maid's suggestion *"You also are one of them."* The response from Peter is instantaneous: *"Man, I am not"* (Lk 22:58). He is defiant but holds his head as a guilty man. He has about one hour to reconsider what he has done. Strangely, he feels less guilty this time. He is sure that there will be no further questioning; after all, he has made himself quite clear. There is, therefore, no chance of a third denial.

Jesus is being kept under guard, awaiting his appearance before the Sanhedrin as soon as it can be convened. He cannot be approached. Then, experiencing something of the shock of a sudden flash of lightening after the storm and danger are believed to have passed, Peter hears: *"Certainly this man was also with him; for he is a Galilean"* (Lk 22:59). Maybe, just prior to this, the speaker caught sight of Jesus. Peter is ready once more with the instant denial: *"Man, I do not know what you are saying."* Immediately he winces and contorts his face as he catches our Lord's eye. He is profoundly sorry and is forgiven.

Of course, in the light of the approaching day and the flickering fire, *we* would have begun to praise the Nazarene, sprung to his defense, and taken issue with his accusers. We would have been proud to associate ourselves with the name of Jesus. In reality, our likely response would have been Peter's response. Of course, the second and third denials are even easier than the first, and the more we deny, the more truthful that denial becomes. Have we then the courage to catch our Lord's eye?

O Lord, forgive our denials, which we in our weakness continually make, and give us the strength and fortitude to say no to Satan's wiles.

Our Father . . . Hail Mary . . . Glory be . . .

STATION 13

Jesus Before the Sanhedrin and the Suicide of Judas

When the day came, the assembly of the elders of the people gathered together, both chief priests and scribes; and they led him away to their council (Luke 22:66–71).

When Judas saw that he [Jesus] was condemned, he repented (Matthew 27:3–10).

The Sanhedrin was probably convened in an assembly room close to the Temple about a quarter of a mile across the lower city.

Within the chamber, there is much questioning and cross-questioning of Jesus before the elders, the chief priests, and the scribes. Jesus points out to them that there is no purpose in pursuing a particular line of examination because their minds are already closed. *"But from now on the Son of Man shall be seated at the right hand of the power of God."* They ask, *"Are you the Son of God, then?"* With a sigh and perhaps even a wry smile, Jesus replies: *"You say that I am"* (Lk 22:70).

Satisfied that Jesus has blasphemed, the council is confident that they will find false witnesses to make a case of treason and sedition to place before the governor, Pontius Pilate.

Judas is present, inside the chamber or outside, but close enough to the proceedings to discover quickly that Jesus is to be taken to the governor's seat of judgment where the verdict is likely to be death. Then, in order to undo the damage he has done, Judas returns to the chief priests the money he was paid. He tries to assure them that Jesus is an innocent man and that the matter is spiraling out of control. From their point of view, however, everything is going according to plan. The matter is out of their hands; Judas can do exactly as he pleases, but there is no hope that any decision will be reversed.

What had Judas expected—an uprising in support of the maligned teacher from Nazareth after his arrest in the Garden of Gethsemane? Had he envisaged the overthrow of the Roman authority in Jerusalem by catching that authority unawares? Judas had played with fire and was about to be responsible for the death of the man he called his friend.

Judas casts down the silver at the feet of the chief priests and hangs himself because he cannot face asking our Lord's forgiveness.

∙⧰⊙⧰∙

By Jesus's sacrifice on the cross the wrongs we have done are already forgiven and we can make amends and restitution with prayer, penance, and good works. Let us learn from the grave error of Judas.

What did the chief priests know of the Son of Man, the Son of God, or the Messiah? They could not see in Jesus their preconception of a divinely-appointed soldier: they had not understood the prophets.

Be none submerged in sin's distress,
None lifted up in boastfulness;
That contrite hearts be not dismayed,
Nor haughty souls in ruin laid.

— *Anonymous, "Magnae Deus potentiae"*
(sixth century)

Our Father . . . Hail Mary . . . Glory be . . .

STATION 14 — *Jesus Before Pilate*

"*Are you the King of the Jews?*" (Matthew 27:11; John 18:33; Luke 23:3)

Pilate seats himself comfortably and waves away an attendant.

"*Are you the King of the Jews?*" Pilate asks Jesus.

"*You have said so,*" replies Jesus politely, perhaps with a slight bow.

A general clamor arises as the elders and the chief priests recklessly hurl about further accusations in the hope of catching the imagination of Pilate.

"*Are you the King of the Jews?*"

"*Do you say this of your own accord, or did others say it to you about me?*"

"*Am I a Jew? Your nation has handed you over to me. . . .*"

"*My Kingship is not of this world. . . .*"

"So you are a king?"

"You say that I am a king . . . I have come into the world to bear witness to the truth. . . ."

"What is truth?"

Pilate is satisfied that there is no threat to him or to the Roman Empire. The fellow is either what he says or is a complete fool; *either way he is no threat to me*, he thinks.

"Are you the King of the Jews?"

"You have said so."

And Pilate said to the chief priests and the multitudes, "I find no crime in this man."

But they were urgent, saying, "He stirs up the people, teaching throughout all Judea, from Galilee even to this place."

When Pilate hears this, he pauses and, perhaps holding up his hand for quiet, asks if Jesus is a Galilean.

This is the break Pilate needs, an excuse to pass the buck. He will play for time and pass this King of the Jews over to Tetrarch Herod Antipas for his opinion. Pilate sees that the crowd is likely to turn ugly. Maybe Herod's view—one way or the other—will appease the crowd.

❧

"Am I a Jew?" Pilate asks. Am I in the least interested in anything but not rocking the boat? Perhaps, but this man seems to be genuine and truthful; but what is truth? The

chief priests will give me their truth, which is another truth altogether, because they know I have no wish to have a riot in the city. Does the King of the Jews have the truth?

What truth is revealed in our lives?

O Heavenly Father, who with your Son sent us the Holy Spirit of Truth, grant that we may remain faithful to the truth of all that you have revealed to us.

Our Father . . . Hail Mary . . . Glory be . . .

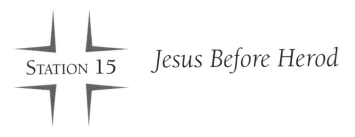

STATION 15 *Jesus Before Herod*

When Pilate heard this, he asked whether the man was a Galilean. And when he learned that he belonged to Herod's jurisdiction, he sent him over to Herod (Luke 23:6, 7).

Pilate believes he may be able to avoid passing sentence on Jesus, or at least avoid responsibility for his death. It is clear that Pilate is uneasy about disposing of Jesus. There may be a backlash. Equally, a riot may ensue if he refuses the demands of the elders of the people. His reputation in Rome is on the line. *Let us pass this King of the Jews over to Herod. The elders will respect his views.* What Pilate desires more than anything is to be able to abdicate his responsibility for any sentence involving Jesus. Are his motives clear to us?

However, Jesus does not answer any question Herod puts to him. Jesus recognizes Herod's shallowness: he knows nothing will be gained by argument. He remains silent. Herod and his court satisfy themselves with a little mockery at the expense of justice as accusations from the chief priests and the scribes fly about in a frenzied demand for blood. They begin to feel, perhaps, that they have lost the initiative. They are concerned that Jesus is now a bargaining chip in the power struggle between Pilate and Herod: they must recover the situation and renew their demand for blood. Herod, who knows that he is as dispensable as Pilate, responds by treating Jesus badly and by parading him in a splendid garment to give the impression of one of the kings of old. In this way he is returned to Pilate. Curiously, even in these circumstances, it is through Jesus that reconciliation is effected between Herod and Pilate.

≈@≈

We open our hearts to the Heavenly Father who already knows our secrets, but how often do we try to hide our motives and intentions from God as Adam and Eve attempted to hide themselves from God in the garden?

Our hearts are open, Lord, to thee:
Thou knowest our infirmity;
Pour out on all who seek thy face
Abundance of thy pardoning grace.

— *Attributed to Saint Gregory the Great,*
"Audi, benign Conditor"

Our Father . . . Hail Mary . . . Glory be . . .

STATION 16

Jesus Again Before Pilate

Pilate then called together the chief priests and rulers and the people, and said to them, "You brought me this man as one perverting the people" (Luke 23:13–19).

Pilate informs the chief priests that he finds in Jesus no fault worthy of a sentence of death. "Why," he says, "I even sent him over to Herod Antipas, and he could not get a confession out of him for any offense whatsoever." But Pilate is now dealing with a crowd incensed. The agents of the chief priests and elders have done their work; they have schooled the mob so well that they shout and bay with one voice. They now smell blood and are determined to have it.

Still Pilate is not happy—even his wife has urged him to spare Jesus (Mt 27:19). To appease the crowd, he reminds them that through his beneficence he allows them to select a prisoner for release at the time of the

Passover. "Perhaps we can settle this now if I give you the King of the Jews as your pardoned prisoner and let that be an end of it." This is a clever move. Wily old Pilate thinks he can hoodwink the chief priests into accepting a guilty verdict provided Jesus is pardoned. The mob will have none of it. "Give us the seditious cutthroat, Barabbas," they cry.

With our Lord's words, *"You would have no power over me unless it had been given you from above; therefore he who delivered me to you has the greater sin,"* ringing in his ears, Pilate makes his final appeals to the crowd. They respond, *"If you release this man, you are not Caesar's friend . . ."* (Jn 19:11, 12). Now these words begin to trouble Pilate again; he does not want that sort of rumor traveling across to Rome. He makes his last attempt: *"Shall I crucify your King?"* And the crowd cries out words unutterable for a proud God-centered nation as they deny God: *"We have no king but Caesar!"* (Jn 19:15). They have pledged their allegiance to the foreign power, their sworn enemy, and rejected the King of Kings. Is Pilate using Jesus to trap the people of Jerusalem into this declaration of allegiance?

◆◆◆◆

Was Pilate guilty of duplicity? Annas, Caiaphas, and the Sanhedrin were guilty of calumny—the building of a case on falsehood by false witnesses. The supporting crowds were even willing to refute their faith at the behest of the chief priests, scribes, and elders by claiming that they were Caesar's rather than God's people, in exchange for the blood of Jesus.

In our everyday lives, gossip is the parent of detraction and calumny. There is no distinction between them.

O Heavenly Father, whose Son was condemned through dishonesty and falsehood for the satisfaction of others, give us the strength and self-control to resist the temptation to seek popularity by these means.

Our Father . . . Hail Mary . . . Glory be . . .

Pilate Washes His Hands

"His blood be on us and on our children!" (Matthew 27:25)

The Barabbas party wins the day, and he is released to the people. *"What shall I do with Jesus who is called Christ?"* asks Pilate. *"Let him be crucified!"* (Mt 27:22) they cry out. Pilate asks them what evil they thought he had done, but the mob does not reason; they have been completely programmed by the officials and agents of the chief priests and scribes, walking among them urging them to demand crucifixion if they know what is good for them.

So they shout all the more for Christ's blood: *"Let him be crucified!"* The frightened men of the temple have done their work, as their predecessors had done with the prophets and messengers of their time. But now the wicked vineyard workers refuse the Son access to his Father's vineyard and they seek to kill him (see Lk 20:9–18). They want it for themselves; theirs is a cozy existence.

And so, with a final shrug of the shoulders and a keen interest in keeping the peace, Pilate acquiesces. He performs one final ceremony before the crowd, in order to show that the decision is entirely theirs. A servant brings to him an elaborate bronze bowl and, lifting a pitcher, pours water over Pilate's hands. With perfunctory ceremony the servant hands a towel to his master. Pilate faces the satisfied and waiting crowd and declares: *"I am innocent of this righteous man's blood; see to it yourselves"* (Mt 27:24). The crowd willingly allows Pilate his innocence; they will happily take upon themselves the burden of this man's death; *"His blood be on us and on our children!"*

What a telling cry! Matthew records that the crowd is content to accept full responsibility for its demands. "Yes, let us be culpable, and let culpability fall upon the future generations; our consciences are clear." What irony this is. As our Lord begins to shed his blood at his scourging, through the *Via Dolorosa* and on Calvary, it does indeed fall upon those in the crowd and upon their children—but not in condemnation. His redeeming blood flows freely as a gift of God's good grace.

❧❀❧

Are we content to wash our hands and convince ourselves of our innocence? Is it as easy as that? Do we always consider the consequences of what we do and say? *"His blood be on us and on our children!"*

Cleanse us, O Lord, from every stain,
Help us the meed of praise to gain,
Till with the Angels linked in love
Joyful we tread thy courts above.

— *Anonymous, "Ecce tempus idoneum"*
(twelfth century)

Our Father . . . Hail Mary . . . Glory be . . .

STATION 18

Jesus Receives His Cross

. . . [A]nd having scourged Jesus, delivered him to be crucified (Matthew 27:26).

With the release of Barabbas, the pardoned man, comes the scourging of the condemned man and the inevitable ritual humiliation.

"Hail, King of the Jews!" they cry, and bow in mock obeisance to Jesus. They kneel before him; they spit on him; they hit him about the head with a cane. They give him the cane as a scepter. This is one of the perks for those on crucifixion detail. They laugh with scorn at the pathetic figure before them and spit again. They dress him up in the cloak that has been placed over his shoulders by Herod's guards. And one ingenious soldier orders a citizen to go to the city wall, a few yards away, where the *Paliurus* bush grows, to collect some twigs. The soldier deftly fashions these into a plaited ring without pricking himself, and with great ceremony presses it firmly upon the head

of Jesus. The thorns tear through the thin flesh of the scalp. The soldiers are pleased with the result and take up their chant once more: *"Hail, King of the Jews!"*

The bullying is infectious and the younger soldiers enter into the spirit of the occasion, doubling their efforts in order to impress their seniors. They attempt to outdo the cruelty of their fellows. Complete with crown, robe, and scepter, our Lord endures the horseplay, which is merely a prelude to greater horrors to come. And when they have laughed enough, the centurion orders them to prepare Jesus and the other prisoners for their march to Golgotha. The costume given to Jesus is removed and his own clothes are returned. He dresses himself, perhaps accompanied by hoots of derision. For good measure our Lord is encouraged to keep his crown; perhaps he is patted on the head to ensure a firmer fit. Do we, at this point, raise our voices against the maltreatment of the prisoners? Probably not.

Can we imagine how the little ceremony of investing the prisoner with his cross might reignite the enthusiasm of the general crowd? Perhaps it is laid over his right shoulder so the tail of the cross drags over the cobbles at a slight angle behind him. The roughness of the timber enrages the wounds already inflicted upon his back. "Heave ho!" some jolly bystander cries, but distraught women and some of our Lord's disciples are also gathering for the start of the procession.

❧❧❧

For good measure, our Lord is probably encouraged to keep his crown. He journeys to his coronation not as the King of the Jews only but as Christ the King, who will reign above the men and women of Golgotha and over humankind.

Forgive us, O Heavenly Father, for the occasions on which we mocked when we ought to have encouraged and derided when we ought to have comforted, and grant that we may always keep before us the image of your suffering Son, our Lord Jesus Christ.

Our Father . . . Hail Mary . . . Glory be . . .

STATION 19

Jesus Falls

And when they had mocked him, they . . . led him away to crucify him (Matthew 27:31).

It is likely that the journey to Golgotha begins at the Antonia Fortress Tower in the northeastern corner of the city, where the crosses are placed upon the shoulders of the condemned men. As we know, two thieves accompany Jesus. Let us suppose they walk one after the other with Jesus in the third place in this sorry caravan.

Although not canonical, the three falls of the traditional fourteen *Stations of the Cross* may be inferred from the fact that Simon is ordered to help Jesus with his cross. And they give pause for more profound contemplation. It is most likely the weight of the cross on his body, weakened by thrashing and other abuse, that causes Jesus to stagger, stumble, and fall. The tail of the cross snags on the cobbles of the street and jars his shoulder as the march begins. It was not unknown for one of the soldiers to place a foot on the timber in order to cause the prisoner to collapse to his knees. Oh yes, there was much fun to be had out of a crucifixion procession. But the centurion— the sergeant-major—wants to keep the column moving, as there are bound to be friends and relations anxious for a final embrace.

As the prisoners begin their journey, how do we react? Close by is the sorrowful figure of Mary, the Mother of Jesus. She gasps amid her tears as she sees her Son sway and fall to one knee, bending low over the cobbles.

❧

The shock of seeing our Lord fall and the sympathy we experience at the sight of Mary's reaction kindles a fire of resentment in us, and we remember that we are called to minister to others in their various needs—the sick and hungry; the sad, the downtrodden and imprisoned. We remember that Christ is in the face of the beggar and in the face of the dying, and that Christ will shine from our faces as we tend their wounds.

O Heavenly Father, whose Son suffered all the pains of his journey to Golgotha, help us when we look at the image of your crucified Son to see the needs of others and respond by means of good works and prayer.

Our Father . . . Hail Mary . . . Glory be . . .

STATION 20

*Jesus Greets
His Mother*

*And there followed him a great multitude of the peo-
ple, and of women who bewailed and lamented him*
(Luke 23:27).

Numbering among the womenfolk are the Galilean
women: Mary of Magdala; Joanna; Susannah; Mary,
the wife of Clopas; and Salome, an aunt of Jesus. Of course
his mother is with them and, maybe, Martha and Mary
from Bethany, and many others. It is inconceivable that
Mary his mother and some others would not attempt to
greet him personally on the way.

Balancing unsurely and unsteadily after his fall, Jesus
presses forward again with a lurching gait. The soldier
behind him encourages him forward. Mary stares at her
staggering son; as she walks alongside, she moves closer
to him with her arms outstretched. Jesus steadies himself,
finding he can use the timber of the cross as a temporary
prop, painful though it is to do so. The woman is

obviously the prisoner's mother, so no one prevents her clutching his arm or interferes with their greeting one another. Even the ill-disciplined soldier behind Jesus has found something else to amuse him.

Their embrace is restricted. Nothing is said: no words are necessary. There are two gulps from our Lady and a deep but quiet moan from Jesus. Briefly each looks into the other's eyes, and they read the thoughts they see. For a moment the world stands still. The other women keep their distance, unwilling to break the spell. "Let's move it now!" This call from the centurion looses the embrace but not the indestructible bond between mother and Son; between Creator and created, between God and his Mother.

᠂ᴬᵒ꒬ᴬ᠂

Does Mary see in his eyes something of both his sorrow and infinite mercy? What does Jesus see in our eyes, and what do we see in his? Indeed, are we able to look our Lord in the eye or does shame prevent any contact?

Thy feet the way of suffering trod;
Thy hand the victory won:
What shall we render to our God
For all that he has done?

— J. M. Neale, *"O Thou Who Through This Holy Week"*

Our Father . . . Hail Mary . . . Glory be . . .

STATION 21

Simon of Cyrene Is Ordered to Assist with the Cross

And they compelled a passer-by, Simon of Cyrene, who was coming in from the country, the father of Alexander and Rufus, to carry his cross (Mark 15:21).

The centurion looks again along the column. The last prisoner is lagging behind, and he sees that the soldiers are once more goading him. Enough is enough! There is sympathy for this prisoner along the way: *There will be no riot on my watch!* The centurion gives orders for the rear-guard soldier to be re-deployed, and he studies our Lord briefly and makes the decision to force someone to carry the tail of the cross.

They are now entering a narrow street beside the north wall of the city. A large man is wedged uneasily in a doorway adjacent to Jesus and the centurion beckons, points, and Simon of Cyrene obeys, stepping from the doorway and raising the timber from the roadway. The jostling crowd, the wailing from the cluster of women keeping pace with Jesus, and the oppressively narrow street alarm him. Simon is a visitor to Jerusalem: he has brought his sons Rufus and Alexander for the Passover. Is he simply lodging in that narrow street?

To be ordered to assist in such a grizzly procession is a daunting prospect. What if he is mistaken for a condemned man and crucified notwithstanding his pleas and protests of innocence? He feels sorry for himself but realizes there is someone in front of him in a far worse situation. He hears a cry from Jesus as he immediately adds weight to the bruised shoulder by lifting the tail of the cross.

By the time Mark writes his account, Simon is known to him along with his two sons. Do we assume that Simon was converted simply by his proximity to Jesus as he walked the Way of the Cross?

If we walk the Way of the Cross, the Way of Duty, the Way of Love, how many will be encouraged to acknowledge Christ by our example?

O Father in Heaven, grant that we may live our lives on earth as though we were in heaven.

Our Father . . . Hail Mary . . . Glory be . . .

STATION 22

Jesus Meets the Woman with the Towel

So they took Jesus, and he went out, bearing his own cross, to the place called the place of a skull, which is called in Hebrew Golgotha (John 19:17).

The non-canonical story of Veronica can be a fertile focus for our attention and contemplation. Was the story an incident remembered and passed on by those who were there? Was she the woman who was cured by the touch of the hem of the Master's garment? No matter her name, let us suppose that she numbered among the women who followed him from Galilee. Although a few incidents along the *Via Dolorosa* were recorded in the Gospels, there must have been many left unrecorded.

There is a strange momentum in the procession, and suddenly into the middle of it steps a naturally timid, self-effacing woman, emboldened by profound indignation at the grievous and grave mistake Pilate and the people have made. She holds a cloth, for she has been mopping her own eyes for some hours. Here she is in the confusion of the moment, overwhelmed with a mixture of anger and devotion, recklessly halting this grim train. But it is not a quiet moment; the people are noisy—some are wailing, others (who have not long ceased yelling "crucify!") are now contributing obscenities. Into this mayhem she steps and lovingly wipes the blood, sweat, and tears from the forehead, eyes, and cheeks of the Savior. For a moment or two the scene seems nothing more than a bad dream. But no, everything is real enough, and with the little ministry complete and gratefully accepted, matters proceed on their inevitable way. Let us imagine that we look through the eyes of this woman. What do we see as we approach our Lord? We see nothing but a bent figure in a filthy garment, his bleeding knee staining it red from the inside. He staggers, straining under the pain and burden of the timber cross. And we have only the memory of his glittering wit, his gentleness, his loving-kindness, his sanctity. He looks but a poor, frightened man. He is the prisoner on death row whom we never see, the beggar beside the road whom we ignore; he is the terrified victim at the mercy of violent men, whom we do not help; his is the hungry and gaunt face on the charity poster we try to forget, the anxious face we blot out of our memory and thought, dying on a bed of pain. We wipe and dab as Veronica did, and we hear the muttered words of grateful thanks.

We meet our Lord in the Blessed Sacrament and we can meet him elsewhere. *"I was a stranger and you welcomed me, I was naked and you clothed me, I was sick and you visited me, I was in prison and you came to me"* (Mt 25:35–36).

> Therefore behold thy Church, O Lord,
> And grace of penitence accord
> To all who seek with generous tears
> Renewal of their wasted years.

> — *Anonymous, "Jesu, quadragenariae"*
> *(ninth century)*

Our Father . . . Hail Mary . . . Glory be . . .

Jesus Falls
a Second Time

*As they were marching out, they came upon a man of
Cyrene, Simon by name* (Matthew 27:32).

The wailing women have made Simon feel ashamed.
He notes that the woman with the towel has now
joined them. He cannot seem to provide stability for the
prisoner. If we are in the crush of bystanders, do we feel
for Simon's predicament? Do we assist? We certainly do
not assist; we try to keep a safe distance and avoid the
attention of the soldiers, particularly the centurion, who
suddenly seems keen to involve people from the crowd.

After the attention of the woman with the towel, the
column is urged on. Indeed, the progress of the two
thieves has been only marginally faster. Grateful for
Veronica's ministry, Jesus sways again and with supreme
effort thrusts his right foot forward. Alas, he sinks to the
ground on his left knee, twisting it badly between two
cobbles. The weight of the cross, no heavier than the

burden of our sin he takes with him to Calvary, does not keep our Lord down for long, and he slowly rises again and begins to press forward after summoning what strength there is left in his weakened body. Simon moves further under the tail of the cross in order to take more of its weight. Very soon they reach the end of the street and see the city wall to their right as their route becomes wider. The women's wails and grief-stricken cries beside Simon grow more intense. He knows that they will soon be unable to resist clutching Jesus and halting the procession once more.

Our Lord is perspiring profusely and drenched in sweat. Flies are attracted to his forehead, to the rivulets of blood issuing from the wounds inflicted by the thorns.

❧

Lent gives us the time to consider this hideous sight and Jesus's physical ordeal. We are able to picture the effects of the pain of our sins. Good works are a help to Christ, but we can easily knock him to one knee with a careless act, remark, or thought.

O Heavenly Father, whose Son trod willingly the path to Golgotha, grant that we may remain aware of how easily our words and actions can cruelly affect others.

Our Father . . . Hail Mary . . . Glory be . . .

STATION 24

Jesus Meets the Women of Jerusalem

And there followed him . . . women who bewailed and lamented him. But Jesus turning to them said, "Daughters of Jerusalem, do not weep for me, but weep for yourselves and for your children" (Luke 23:27, 28).

Our Lord is no steadier on his feet as the procession moves on. The two thieves are not troubled or comforted by the women of Jerusalem: the women have kept pace with Jesus. They have exchanged greetings with the other women and move themselves closer to the struggling figure, directing their anguish toward him. Is there comfort in the sorrow of others? Perhaps there is. How do we greet Jesus on the way to Calvary? Are these women "official" mourners desirous of pointing to the prisoner's errors, or are they more of his acquaintances and followers?

"Daughters of Jerusalem, do not weep for me, but weep for yourselves and for your children. For behold, the days are coming when they will say, 'Blessed are the barren, and the wombs that never bore, and the breasts that never gave suck!' Then they will begin to say to the mountains, 'Fall on us' and to the hills 'Cover us.' For if they do this when the wood is green, what will happen when it is dry?"

Barrenness was believed to be clear evidence of divine displeasure. To arrive at a time when the situation is worse than living under the anger of God, or at a time when you are in constant fear for your children, is a devastating prediction. Is this a prediction of the sacking of Jerusalem in A.D. 70? No, like Hosea before him, whose words are here quoted and modified by Jesus for effect, he is urging the women to look to themselves and to focus on their lives to see the answer to and cause of their misery. There is not a moment to lose—the "green" wood is the here and now; the "dry" wood is the unknown future.

※

Yet there is hope. Indeed, there is every reason for hope. We, of course, use the discipline of this exercise for our spiritual well-being in the certain knowledge of our Lord's resurrection and of our own salvation. The women of Jerusalem on the *Via Dolorosa* do not have that strength, that advantage. Who can doubt that our Lord's words have an immediate effect? Does the rather self-absorbed wailing cease? Do the words of Jesus cause them to stop and think about his teaching? Can they now see that they are part of salvation history?

The law and seers that were of old
In divers ways this Lent foretold,
Which Christ, all seasons' King and guide,
In after ages sanctified.

— *Attributed to Saint Gregory the Great,*
"Ex more docti mystico"

Our Father . . . Hail Mary . . . Glory be . . .

STATION 25

Jesus Falls a Third Time

They seized one Simon of Cyrene . . . and laid on him the cross, to carry it behind Jesus (Luke 23:26).

The weight of the cross brings Jesus crashing to his knees, and he is pinned to the place where he has fallen. His preparation is over; he has been tested to the breaking point; he will now with certainty be able to bear the weight of humanity's sin as he hangs at Golgotha. As Jesus falls to his knees this third time, cries of alarm from his Mother and Mary Magdalene pierce the air and, again, their arms extend toward the fallen figure; but they can do no good. Joanna and Susannah clutch one another in mutual support. For the few remaining steps of the journey, Simon, now with confidence and a sense of vocation, carries the cross behind Jesus. This too is our lesson.

Jesus's head is racked with pain—a violent migraine, caused by the cumulative effects of the events of the day and by the thorns now embedded in his skull, throbs violently and relentlessly. And now as the rear of the column rounds the northwestern corner of the city, it approaches the gate that looks over Golgotha, the place of the skull.

Crucifixion is most certainly not a daily event here, and the curious are there with the ill-wishers, along with the devoted followers and those whose lives have been touched in some way or other by our Lord.

His bloodied knees and back have damaged his tunic somewhat, though the soldiers will be content to bid and throw dice for any of his possessions.

> *And he said to all, "If any man would come after me, let him deny himself and take up his cross daily and follow me. For whoever would save his life will lose it; and whoever loses his life for my sake, he will save it" (Lk 9:23, 24).*

⁂

Grant, O Heavenly Father, that we may ever follow the saints who selflessly carried their crosses behind your Son, our Savior.

Our Father . . . Hail Mary . . . Glory be . . .

Jesus Arrives at Golgotha

And when they came to a place called Golgotha (which means the place of a skull), they offered him wine to drink, mingled with gall; but when he tasted it, he would not drink it (Matthew 27:33–34).

Framed by the gateway, the rise of Golgotha awaits its three principal guests. It has held many crosses— crosses for murderers, crosses for seditious criminals, crosses for thieves, crosses for enemies of the state, even crosses for lesser crimes. Never before has it held a cross for the King of the Jews.

As the prisoners and their fellow travelers squeeze through the gate, they are confronted by a large gathering already assembled, skirting the crest of the hill. There are shaft pits lined with wood into which—if all goes well— the crosses will slide: the great wooden wedges rest beside them, ready to lock and secure the crosses upright. A civilian in a leather apron waits to carry out his grizzly duties; his task is to fix the prisoners firmly to the timber. He must choose the appropriate nails for the limb on which he is working. He must take note of the weight of the prisoner; an extra block and rope may be necessary. It is not a daily chore for this man: he is able to handle most things.

A few canes stand in a disused cross socket, discarded sponges beside them. The place is rocky with a little sandy soil and a few tussocks of coarse grass growing here and there. Blood stains the surface of the hill, and swarms of ever-present flies anxious for sustenance buzz around the ground. There is a broken waterpot filled with sour wine and gall (an opiate) propped up by a finely-shaped stone, a relic of a prestigious building long gone. The prisoners are encouraged to drink the foul cocktail, as it dulls the senses and makes them easier to handle.

He who was born of Mary, who came down from heaven, is to be dispatched from the top of this frightening place. And yet, it is now a place of forgiveness, of redemption, of unconditional love.

O loving wisdom of our God!
When all was sin and shame,
A second Adam to the fight
And to the rescue came.
O wisest love! That flesh and blood

Which did in Adam fail,
Should strive afresh against their foe,
Should strive and should prevail.

— *Blessed J. H. Newman, "The Dream of Gerontius"*

Our Father . . . Hail Mary . . . Glory be . . .

STATION 27 *Jesus Is Stripped and Nailed to the Cross*

There they crucified him, and with him two others, one on either side, and Jesus between them (John 19:18).

Now the soldiers can have their fun. They can strip their prisoners with some ceremony and entertain most of the crowd with their fine ribald wit. True, there are always the families and friends there, but they are usually too busy wailing to notice. The chief priests and scribes are not impressed with the common jests of the soldiers but are there to make sure they see the last of Jesus of Nazareth.

Jesus and the thieves are pushed toward their appointed positions and stripped before the crowd. Christ is laid bare as at Bethlehem. Having arrived from the Heavenly Father through Mary, he now prepares to return through his willing sacrifice in exchange for the redemption of humanity. But the soldiers and the crowd are not interested in the theology of it all, even had they known it; they see a man whose simple possessions are now the subject of squabble, the throw of the dice, and of triumph.

With that part of the show now over, the prisoners are made to lie on their crosses. The man with the leather apron secures the thieves to their crosses on either side of Jesus, and slightly behind him. The disciple John, Salome, and the other women remain a little way from the top of the hill; the Mother of Jesus feels obliged to be close to her Son as with grim accuracy and skill the arms are fixed through the palm of each hand at such an angle that the long nail enters the wood from the wrist. Larger nails are selected for the feet, which are placed one on top of the other. The nails are driven through the feet, so recently bathed by Mary of Bethany, into the cross and down into the foot block. The hammer blows thrust yet another sword through Mary's soul.

We find it easy to visualize this horror, but let us concentrate our thoughts for a moment on those hands. Those hands that have healed and touched the beggar and the blind man, the dead man and the dumb, are now fixed to rough, un-planed timber in such grievous pain only to be guessed at.

O generous love! That He who smote
In man for man the foe,
The double agony in man
For man should undergo.

— *Blessed J. H. Newman, "The Dream of Gerontius"*

Our Father . . . Hail Mary . . . Glory be . . .

STATION 28

The Indictment

Pilate also wrote a title and put it on the cross; it read, "Jesus of Nazareth, the King of the Jews" (John 19:19).

The cry of the prisoners has dropped to a gentle moan. Now the indictments prepared after their sentencing are fixed above the heads of the condemned. Those guilty of theft are, quite simply, named as thieves. However, the chief priests are astonished when the plaque is handed to the carpenter to place on the cross of Jesus. They take issue and one returns to Pilate to ask that he amend the wording. Pilate is adamant: *"What I have written I have written."*

The plaques are already in place and the crosses are now roped, hauled up into position and wedged. The prisoners groan as the weight of their bodies tugs at their wrists and hands. The raising of the crosses has reanimated most of the crowd, who, delighted at the spectacle, accompany the procedure with a raucous "Heave-ho!"

The indictments are clear for all to see, announced in Hebrew for the sake of the educated Jew; Latin for the officials of the Roman authorities and their records; and Greek for the information of everyman. This vulgar Greek is the common language of most of the Roman Empire, and those of Jerusalem and the Aramaic speakers of Galilee and of the countryside understand it. Soon, all who happen by see that here hangs Jesus of Nazareth, the King of the Jews.

The chief priests are satisfied at the spectacle of Jesus on the cross: they are angry, however, that he remains described as *"Jesus of Nazareth, the King of the Jews."*

Fulfilled is all that David told
In true prophetic song of old;
Amidst the nations, God, said he,
Hath reigned and triumphed from the tree.

— *Venantius Fortunatus, "Vexilla Regis prodeunt"*
(sixth century)

Our Father . . . Hail Mary . . . Glory be . . .

STATION 29

Jesus Suffers the Taunts of the Bystanders

And those who passed by derided him, wagging their heads, and saying, "Aha! You who would destroy the temple and build it in three days, save yourself, and come down from the cross!" So also the chief priests mocked him to one another with the scribes, saying, "He saved others; he cannot save himself. Let the Christ, the King of Israel, come down now from the cross, that we may see and believe." Those who were crucified with him also reviled him (Mark 15:29–32).

Not content with the gruesome procedure that sees a prisoner humiliated in the streets, in terrible agony as he is nailed to and drawn up on the cross, tormented by the persistent and unmerciful flies with his arms stretched beyond endurance, the bystanders continue with their taunts, their chanting, and their abuse.

If the man on the cross is a thief, the passer-by might scoff, sneer, and spit. Unless he is the victim of that thief, that is the end of it. In the case of Jesus matters are different. In the eyes of the chief priests and scribes he is, at the very least, a blasphemer and has threatened their relatively comfortable lifestyle. He has "rocked the boat." He is not the Christ, the Messiah, and most certainly not the King of the Jews. And yet, staring down at them with his crown of thorns is this Jesus of Nazareth, a notice above his head officially declaring that he is the King of the Jews. The ire of the temple officials cannot be silenced!

The passers-by join with the jeering chief priests and, astonishingly, so do the two thieves. There is some comfort in being on the same side; perhaps they have no friends to be with them in their last hours and seek camaraderie elsewhere. One of the thieves is less enthusiastic and begins to think.

What makes men shout abuse at those in no position to retaliate? Is it guilt or envy? Is their anger really directed at themselves? Are we jeered at or mocked on account of our faith? Perhaps we keep it so well hidden that no one knows that we are followers of Christ. Should not our lives make it obvious that we are?

O Heavenly Father, grant that even by the way we behave others may come to be reconciled with you through your Son.

Our Father . . . Hail Mary . . . Glory be . . .

STATION 30

The First Word from the Cross

"Father, forgive them for they know not what they do"
(Luke 23:34).

W as this most significant plea to the Heavenly Father spoken as the soldiers hauled the cross above the onlookers? And was it a plea on behalf of those who had nailed him to the cross, who had sentenced him, who had condemned him, who had lied on the witness stand; a plea for Judas, for Annas and Caiaphas, for Herod Antipas and Pilate? Oh yes, without a doubt, but it was more far-reaching than anyone could have imagined.

"Father, forgive them," for your creatures are crafted in your own image. The guilt of Adam's sin of pride (the mother of all sin) through the ages and into the future weighs heavily on them. I am able to take that sin upon myself, in accordance with your will; I am able to carry its weight, which will be crucified with me, the necessary

sacrifice, the scapegoat and lamb together. In addition, *"Father, forgive them"* their past and future sin as I also assume its burden and so free humanity through the Church I leave behind, nourished by the blood I now shed for the world. *"Father, forgive them for they know not what they do!"*

Jesus's friends and relations keep their distance. Some think they will soon awake from the nightmare, but of course they do not awake. We stand with them and see the Master high above, with the diminutive figure of Mary alone at his feet. Just over the wall, city life is carrying on much as usual; here there is nothing but profound misery. What is running through the Beloved Disciple's mind as he considers moving forward, up the hill, to join our Lady? Unknown to him, though it will slowly dawn on him, God's great plan for the salvation of humanity is all but complete. With Jesus's plea to the Heavenly Father, the contract is signed, sealed, and settled, and in a moment the ransom will be paid.

⋆⊛⋆

As our Lord suffers the hideous torture of the cross, the pain of our sin and of the consequences of that sin, he cries out and pleads for our absolution!

Pride is the worship of self. How often do we satisfy that desire by placing ourselves before our duty to God and our neighbor?

Heavenly Father, who through your Son has blotted out the sin of Adam and Eve and has sealed for us that abundant grace in our Baptism, grant that though we are free to commit the sin of pride afresh, we may, when tempted, ever bring to mind your crucified Son.

Our Father . . . Hail Mary . . . Glory be . . .

STATION 31

The Second Word from the Cross

"Truly, I say to you, today you will be with me in Paradise" (Luke 23:43).

What a reply to receive amid the aggressive noise of the occasion—the ribaldry of the soldiers, the derisive laughter of the officials, the mockery of the crowds in which both thieves have joined. They think they can gain some sort of temporary companionship with the crowds by siding with them in their abuse of Jesus. But one thief suddenly turns on his fellow when he realizes he is about to die. He has placed himself before everything during his life; he has stolen at will and has never thought of anyone else. He tries to help his companion to see the reality of their situation: *"Do you not fear God, since you are under the same sentence . . . ? And we indeed justly; for we are receiving the due reward of our deeds; but this man has done nothing wrong. Jesus, remember me when you come in your kingly power"* (Lk 23:40–42). The thief asks for nothing other than to be *remembered*. How does Jesus respond? What is bound up in his reply?

"You have changed course at the eleventh hour; the Heavenly Father especially loves the wayward sheep who returns to the fold, even if he is very late. The angels in heaven are rejoicing as we speak! You ask me to remember you, to think of you, to pray for you, to intercede for you, but I will lavish upon you much more than that. The Heavenly Father's generosity knows no bounds. *"Truly, I say unto you, today you will be with me in Paradise."*

We are some distance from the cross, standing with Salome and her son, John, the Beloved Disciple, with Mary, the wife of Clopas, and other acquaintances. Even so, we manage to hear this extraordinary exchange between the thief on the left and the Master. We see our Lord smile, even in his agony: we are amazed at the loving Father's power to transform, to effect change. One moment the thief is tormenting Jesus along with the soldiers, the next he is acknowledging his sinfulness and the justice of his punishment. He recognizes the purity and perfection of Jesus's sacrifice because he attests the Lord's innocence. The thief's request is modest; his reward sublime.

✦

Following his cry for forgiveness for everyone, Jesus now shows divine forgiveness in action. The thief is the first to experience the saving power of the Crucified.

God's mercy is infinite, and he does not tire of forgiving. What can be more comforting to us?

Merciful God, your Son Jesus Christ gave us the parables of the lost sheep and the lost coin, and he told us of the men hired from the marketplace at the eleventh hour; let us know your loving kindness and mercy as we repent and change the course of our lives.

Our Father . . . Hail Mary . . . Glory be . . .

STATION 32

The Third Word from the Cross

"Woman, behold your son! . . . Behold, your mother!"
(John 19:26–27)

O ur Lord sees that John is there and perhaps asks him to come forward to join his Mother Mary at the foot of the cross. He has something specific to say to them. Throughout his ministry he has looked after the two sons of Salome (Mary's sister), particularly the younger of the two, at the insistence of his aunt. Now, as Jesus has no family of his age closer than his cousins, the time has come to make sure his Mother will be looked after for the rest of her earthly life. It is the inevitable last thought of a dutiful Son.

"Woman, behold your son!" My duties to you on earth are now John's duties; the care I have given him during my ministry he will now lavish upon you, my dear Mother. And John, you whom I named, with James, the "Thunder Boys," you must look lovingly upon my Mother as yours. *"Behold, your mother!"*

As John leaves the cluster in which we stand and moves forward to the cross, we see that he is representing us as the Church, taking on the blissful duty of respect and honor and love for Mary, the Mother of God. By his words, our Lord places the Church in his Mother's care, thereby confirming her as Mother of the Church. We are to become to her as devoted sons and daughters; she must have a special place in our affections. In turn, Mary, as loving Mother, will intercede for us now and at the hour of our death.

As we are called so specifically to become the Church, to be the body of Jesus, our vocation is to reveal Christ to others in the way we care for those less fortunate than ourselves. Whatever our skills and wealth, they are to be used for the benefit of others.

Is it not sobering that the reputation of the Church in the eyes of the world depends upon how we behave and live our lives?

O God, who humbled himself to be born of the Virgin Mary and exalted her to become the Mother of your Church, grant that we may ever love her and dutifully reveal your Son to others by the way in which we live.

Our Father . . . Hail Mary . . . Glory be . . .

STATION 33

The Fourth Word from the Cross

"My God, my God, why hast thou forsaken me?"
(Matthew 27:46; Mark 15:34)

This is a cry of a desperate and downcast man. But is our Lord overcome by the agony of loneliness? Certainly he suffers all the physical feelings and emotions a human can experience in such a prolonged and lingering death. With the combination of his significant loss of blood, the heat of the day, the severely parched mouth, the pain of his wounds, and his inability to fill his lungs with air, he experiences an enshrouding despair. His eyes are unable to focus properly by this stage and he is close to death. The crown—that exquisite item of mockery—is actually fixed to his head by the downward pointing thorns. The pain from his hands and feet, pierced and out of joint, rises through his arms and legs in waves and surges and throbs. Yes, his agony is real enough.

"My God, my God, why hast thou forsaken me?" Yes, Heavenly Father, the psalmist knew despair and this, together with all his other trials, I feel and experience for myself. But he knew also that you are holy and that his forefathers trusted you to deliver them. *"But thou, O Lord, be not far off! O thou my help, hasten to my aid!"* (Ps 22[21]:19). *"My God, my God, why hast thou forsaken me?"*

We hear Jesus begin Psalm 22[21] and consider the parallels it draws between the desperation of the psalmist and the sufferings our Lord is enduring. As the psalmist wrestles with the apparent contradiction of a Messiah who is also the Suffering Servant depicted by Isaiah (Is 53:3–6), we know this is a stumbling block for many of his followers, not least Peter himself. But it is clear that Jesus cannot carry away the burden of our sin without suffering. And yet the psalm goes on to tell us: *"He has not hid his face from him when he cried to him."* Jesus knows the psalm well enough and how it ends in triumph and joy.

The future is attractive and we can be full of hope when we consider what the bountiful God has done for humanity. We have the advantage over those bystanders, for we have a joyful confidence in Christ's glorious resurrection.

O Christ our King, as you reign from the tree, help us to fulfill our vocation to reveal your face to "all the ends of the earth" so that "all the families of nations shall worship."

Our Father . . . Hail Mary . . . Glory be . . .

STATION 34

The Fifth Word from the Cross

"I thirst" (John 19:28).

The provision of sour wine and gall—juice from the seeds of the *papaver somniferum*—at Golgotha was, in a sense, one of benevolence. Taking the mixture calmed the condemned man, dulled his senses, and, as a consequence, made him easier to handle. Our Lord refused the offer of the drink on arrival at Golgotha but later, as time was running out and he could barely move his lips and tongue, he uttered the words, *"I thirst."*

"I thirst." My mouth is parched as I near the end of my life. As I yearn for moisture to aid my dying breath, so I yearn for you, Heavenly Father. The psalmist declared long ago: *"As a hart longs for the flowing streams, so longs my soul for thee. . . . My soul thirsts for God, for the living God"* (Ps 42). *I thirst* too for the salvation of humanity, and it is that thirst which gives me the strength to fulfill your will, Heavenly Father.

Standing rather rigidly and anxiously with the others on the hillside, it begins to dawn on us that a yearning or thirst for God is the supernatural response to the Creator's gift of life. We know Jesus is near his end, and we are shocked at his barely audible, feeble request for the foul liquid kept there in a large, broken urn. Some honorable man runs with the sponge soaked in the wine and offers it on the point of a stick. Of course, this liquid cannot quench his thirst any more than our feeble response to God, for his generosity in showering us with sanctifying grace, will quench his thirst. And, yes, God *does* thirst, as Saint Gregory Nazianzen instructs us in his much thought about and telling phrase, *God thirsts to be thirsted for.* The Creator's gift of life and of a Savior are evidence of that thirst.

@

Even with plenty of water, a land without God is arid, barren, and dry.

As we look on the face of our dying Savior, can we deny him the Creator's thirst to be thirsted for? But how can we thirst for him when most of our attention is devoted to our own well-being and comfort?

God of heaven and earth, give us the grace and strength to respond to you as you would have us respond, through our Lord and Savior.

Our Father . . . Hail Mary . . . Glory be . . .

STATION 35

The Sixth Word from the Cross

"*It is finished*" (John 19:30).

With these words, Jesus begins to breathe his last faltering breaths. Jesus, in his preparation in Gethsemane for the final stage of his mission, accepts the burden of the world's sin, which he will bear along with the cross and the pain. Hanging on the cross, Jesus surveys his friends and relations close at hand—the city and the lands farther afield—as the Creator looked upon his creation in the ages before. He begins his farewell to them: his final breath has to be taken as the earthly task is over, complete; it is accomplished. (This task was conceived before all worlds—and was ever the *divine intention*—before the orbs and spheres were made, before the Big Bang, or in whatever way the Creator formed our solar system and the universe before that. This *divine intention*—the Word—*was with* God before his creative notions made his thoughts matter.)

"*It is finished.*" My work is complete, O Heavenly Father, and it remains for me now to shed my life on earth and prepare the path toward you that the redeemed and ransomed souls will take when they follow me.

We patiently observe: we have not strayed from our vantage point. We have often sung the *Stabat Mater* but have never managed to picture the scene so vividly. There is the tiny figure of our Lady, dwarfed by the cruelty of the cross. Does Mary catch her breath as we hear "*it is finished*"? The unexpectedly loud cry from our Lord's lips certainly startles the rest of the faithful band and sends a shiver down the spine. We take time to observe Golgotha, as the Heavenly Father's momentous action draws to a close. Two soldiers now talk quietly, their raucousness abated. Apart, but not indifferent, stands the centurion. Some of his men search for a handy implement with which to finish off the dying men, should such work be necessary; another of his men stands with a lance. A crow flutters to the pot of wine, disdains to drink, and flies off heavily. Blood has collected beneath the crosses and the sun has rendered it the color of the soldiers' cloaks and the cloth of rank worn by some of the temple officials. Many watch from a greater distance lest they be defiled by dead bodies. They are all actors in this drama; they do not know that they are about to be ransomed and set free.

✦

That the death of the Son of God brings about the salvation of humanity is both a mystery and also evidence of the immeasurable might of the Heavenly Father.

We are made in God's image; so do we not now have the face of God himself, the face that Jesus has given to the Heavenly Father?

God of all creation, help us to understand our place in your plan, and give us the grace to behave as you would have us behave. May we reveal something of your Son in our very faces, and may we recognize him in the faces of others. Amen.

Our Father . . . Hail Mary . . . Glory be . . .

STATION 36

The Seventh Word from the Cross

"Father, into thy hands I commit my spirit!" (Luke 23:46)

Now that every prophecy has been fulfilled, and everything foretold about Jesus is apparent, Jesus returns naturally to the psalms for a quotation to accompany his departure from Golgotha. Soon that sorrowful death of the long-awaited Messiah, now a convicted criminal, will turn to triumph, for the grave will be vanquished for all of us, for all time. Nonetheless, at the time of his death, no joy is felt, and happiness seems far away. It is left to the pagan centurion—a rough, down-to-earth sergeant-major—to leave the scene on a note of hope. *"Certainly this man was innocent"* (Lk 23:47); *"Truly this man was the Son of God!"* (Mk 15:39) are perceptive comments uttered by the man in charge of the execution of the sentence. Instinctively he knows that this man is no criminal; he has seen every kind of criminal. But it is much more than this.

"*Into thy hand I commit my spirit*" (Ps 31[30]:5). There, the psalmist has again spoken for me, O Heavenly Father; they are my last words before I return to you by way of death—that portal so feared. That fear I shall soon expunge. The psalmist foresaw this triumph in his very next words and speaks on behalf of his fellows: "*You have redeemed me, O Lord, faithful God*" (Ps 31[30]:5). He gives you thanks in anticipation of this salvation. "*Father, into thy hand I commit my spirit.*"

Our Lady knows the psalm; she has not wavered in her faith since the day she committed herself to God's plan thirty-odd years ago. Dear old Simeon predicted her seven great sorrows, and she has now suffered her fifth. She remains at the foot of the cross with John. Mary's sister and sister-in-law linger along with Mary of Magdala and other friends—Joanna and Susannah too. We are among them. The emptiness and darkness, grief and sorrow, are tangible.

――

In the seven words from the cross we have a summary of our hope and confidence in the saving power of Christ. His arms are outstretched with the embrace of salvation.

Do our petty trials compare with our experience of Golgotha? With our Lady's example in mind, how easily does our resolution crumble to dust?

Blessed and Holy Trinity, three Persons in one Almighty God, grant us the steadfastness of the Mother of God and the willpower to place our lives in your hands so that we may not succumb to our own desires.

Our Father . . . Hail Mary . . . Glory be . . .

STATION 37

Jesus Dies on the Cross

And Jesus cried again with a loud voice and yielded up his spirit (Matthew 27:50).

Jesus has spoken seven times from the cross. He is given the wine he refused on arrival at Golgotha, and dies. He breathes his last and dies the death of a human. He gives the Heavenly Father a human face, albeit the face of the Suffering Servant. After the physical tests—his arrest, his being struck, his scourging, his arduous journey with the cross, his humiliation, his further agonies, and the effort of his seven dying words from the cross—he dies. In dying the ransom is paid. He has been offered up by the people, but he makes the sacrifice willingly, thereby taking the responsibility away from those who condemned him. Not only has he set humanity free—free from the imprisonment of their sin—but his dying releases his broken body and his blood to become the Body and Blood of the Eucharist. He thus remains physically with his people and sustains them through Holy Church in the form of the Most Holy and Blessed Sacrament.

Those who have by now moved forward to the foot of the cross to join Mary are given some relief knowing his agonies are over, but, at the same time, are saddened to the core of their being at his death and ignominious end. Despair walks closely with sorrow, and yet Mary has not wavered since she accepted God's commission all those years before.

Jesus remains physically with his people. Let us not take the gift of the Blessed Sacrament for granted. Our Lord is in the tabernacle as truly as he was in the manger at Bethlehem and hanging on the tree at Golgotha.

On whose dear arms, so widely flung,
The weight of this world's ransom hung:
The price of humankind to pay,
And spoil the spoiler of his prey.

— *Venantius Fortunatus, "Vexilla Regis prodeunt"*
(sixth century)

Our Father . . . Hail Mary . . . Glory be . . .

STATION 38 *The Side of Jesus Is Pierced*

But when they came to Jesus and saw that he was already dead, they did not break his legs. But one of the soldiers pierced his side with a spear, and at once there came out blood and water. He who saw it has borne witness (John 19:33–35).

The centurion utters his pronouncement for those nearby to hear. He has been uneasy about this man throughout his duty that day. This man, he thinks, may have been who his followers claimed he was. Just look at him; that is not the face of a criminal. *"Truly, this man was the Son of God!"*

When the apostles and evangelists re-read the psalms after the crucifixion, the utterances contained in them burst with new meaning. The crucifixion psalm (Ps 22[21]) seems to follow the last stages of our Lord's passion. *"I am poured out like water, and all my bones are out of joint . . . they have pierced my hands and my feet—I can count all my bones—they stare and gloat over me; they divide my garments among them, and for my raiment they cast lots."* No bones were broken, but his flesh was certainly pierced and his body battered and bruised. His shoulders were probably out of joint, as were—it is most likely—his ankle and toe joints. He died from asphyxia, weakened by the loss of blood.

The soldiers ensure the three criminals are dead. The thieves linger on at the doorway of death, and to hasten their end, the soldiers break their legs with a length of hardwood or an iron bar. Now they can no longer push on their feet to gulp a little air into their restricted lungs. They die quickly from asphyxia and shock. The King of the Jews is dead but the soldiers must make sure all three are dead. They do not bother with the legs of Jesus. Instead, for good measure, one thrusts his lance between two ribs and up into the heart of Jesus. John is close to this final insult and testifies to it. Is he reminded immediately of the miracle at Cana in Galilee and the mysterious outpouring of water into wine? What he is keen to establish is that at this point our Lord is dead beyond any doubt, his human life incapable of resuscitation.

❧❦❧

The King of the Jews is dead. At last, the chief priests and scribes and elders are satisfied and turn away from the hill smiling to themselves and to each other. But they ought to be smiling—they have just been saved.

Where deep for us the spear was dyed,
Life's torrent rushing from his side,
To wash us in that precious flood,
Where mingled Water flowed, and Blood.

— *Venantius Fortunatus, "Vexilla Regis prodeunt"*
(sixth century)

With the outpouring of your love comes salvation. O Sacred Heart of Jesus, have mercy.

Our Father . . . Hail Mary . . . Glory be . . .

STATION 39

Jesus Is Taken from the Cross and Laid in His Mother's Arms

After this, Joseph of Arimathea, who was a disciple of Jesus, but secretly, for fear of the Jews, asked Pilate that he might take away the body of Jesus, and Pilate gave him leave. So he came and took away his body (John 19:38).

It is not difficult to imagine that Mary, the Mother of Jesus, together with her companions in grief, linger there by the cross until Joseph manages to obtain permission to take the body in order to prevent its burial in a place of general interment. Nicodemus, another high ranking but careful disciple, assists. They will make use of a newly-fashioned tomb nearby for the body. In any case, Pilate has agreed to respect the Jewish codes and have all bodies removed from public view before the end of the day. Carefully and not without difficulty, the weight of the body is taken in willing hands and strong arms, removed and carefully lowered to the ground where Mary awaits, ready to cradle the body in her arms as she cradled the tiny child in Bethlehem. Seated on the ground, Mary holds the head and shoulders of this pathetic corpse in her loving arms, her tears washing the blood from the wounds on his forehead. Perhaps, at this stage, Nicodemus gently lifts away the crown of thorns.

A sixth sword is thrust into Mary's soul and the seventh sword of sorrow, predicted by Simeon in the temple, will follow soon.

So it is over. Soon the body of Jesus will be sealed away and will crumble to dust, along with all the hopes and confidence of the disciples. Perhaps Mary alone nurses the seed of hope and expectation but buried beneath her many woes.

The royal banners forward go;
The Cross shines forth in mystic glow;
Where he in flesh, our flesh who made,
Our sentence bore, our ransom paid.

— *Venantius Fortunatus, "Vexilla Regis prodeunt"*
(sixth century)

Our Father . . . Hail Mary . . . Glory be . . .

Jesus Is Laid in the Tomb

Now in the place where he was crucified there was a garden, and in the garden a new tomb where no one had ever been laid. So because of the Jewish day of Preparation, as the tomb was close at hand, they laid Jesus there (John 19:41–42).

And here we are not many yards from the crest of Golgotha, now largely deserted. Here we walk with the body of Jesus to the tomb. It must be done quickly. Nicodemus has brought spices and linen, but there is little time for the proper rituals. They will have to be done after the Sabbath, the day after tomorrow. There is, however, time enough to wrap the head properly and enshroud the body in clean linen. The women agree to return after the Sabbath to complete the work. For a moment or two, they cluster around the small entrance to the tomb and recall the lively wit of Jesus, the absurd hyperbole that got to the very center of what he was illustrating, the antics, the banter with the crowds as he preached, the loving compassion for the lazy and the sick and the sinful, the firmness he showed in the schooling of his close disciples. Each one at the entrance to the tomb holds his or her special memory; but our Lady's memory is most complete, for she has stored up in her mind her Son's whole life, the life she vowed to bring into being to fulfill a plan she understood incompletely.

Nicodemus and Joseph of Arimathea roll the stone into place along the trench in front of the entrance to the tomb, and so close the door on the passion of our Lord.

Is there despair, a feeling of abandonment? Is there anger? Undoubtedly there is sorrow, and despair is a close relation. Is there emptiness? Is there a feeling that all is now lost? Or, deep down, is there a feeling of hope, of expectation? Yes, the seeds sown by our Lord will soon burst into life in the brilliant light of his glorious resurrection.

But now let every heart prepare,
By sacrifice of fast and prayer,
To keep with joy magnifical
The solemn Easter festival.

— *Anonymous, "Jesu, quadragenariae"*
(ninth century)

O Heavenly Father, as we prepare for the celebration of the most glorious feast, may we, by the cross and passion of your Son, be bathed in the glory of his resurrection.

Our Father . . . Hail Mary . . . Glory be. . .

Appendix

The "Expanded" Paternoster

Our Father, who art in heaven, hallowed be thy name.

> O Heavenly Father, praise and thanks for your
> goodness, kindness, and mercy; for your great gifts
> lavished on me, in particular for _____; for the
> glimpses of heaven I see on earth; for the lives of the
> saints and their intercession.

Thy Kingdom come, Thy will be done on earth as it is in
heaven.

> Help me live on earth as though a citizen of heaven.
> Encourage me to be unselfish, and assist me to be an
> instrument of your divine generosity and an agent of
> peace and loving-kindness. Give me the strength to
> fulfill the vocation you have given me.

Give us this day our daily bread.

> Give me only what I need, but look with love on my
> family and friends . . . ; relieve and comfort the sick,

dying and bereaved . . . ; look mercifully upon the souls of the faithful departed.

And forgive us our trespasses, as we forgive those who trespass against us.

Forgive those who sin in ignorance and those for whom I have been an occasion of sin. Forgive my sins of negligence and commission . . . ; forgive me when I fail to forgive others.

And lead us not into temptation, but deliver us from evil. Amen.

Preserve me from temptation . . . and from every evil. . . . Grant these prayers through Christ our Lord. Amen.

Bibliography

Anonymous. "Jesu, quadragenariae [O Jesu Christ, From Thee Began]" in *The English Hymnal*, translated by T. A. Lacey. London: Oxford University Press, 1906.

———. "Magnae Deus potentiae [Almighty God Who From the Flood]" in *The Hymnal Noted*, translated by J. M. Neale. London: Joseph Masters, 1864.

———. "Ecce tempus idoneum [Now Is the Healing Time Decreed]" in *The English Hymnal*, translated by T. A. Lacey. London: Oxford University Press, 1906.

Neale, J. M. "O Thou Who Through This Holy Week" in *The English Hymnal*, translated by J. M. Neale. London: Oxford University Press, 1906.

Newman, Blessed J. H. *The Dream of Gerontius*. London: Macmillan, 1869.

[Saint Gregory the Great]. "Audi, benign Conditor [O Merciful Creator, Hear!]" in *The English Hymnal*, translated by T. A. Lacey. London: Oxford University Press, 1906.

_____. "Ex more docti mystico [The Fast as Taught by Holy Lore]" in *The Hymnal Noted*, translated by J. M. Neale. London: Joseph Masters, 1864.

Saint Thomas Aquinas. "Pange, lingua gloriosi Corporis mysterium [Sing, My Tongue]" in *The English Hymnal*, translated by J. M. Neale. London: Oxford University Press, 1906. N.B. May be called: *Of the Glorious Body Telling*.

Venantius Fortunatus "Vexilla Regis prodeunt [The Royal Banners Forward Go]" in *The Handbook to the Lutheran Hymnal*, translated by J. M. Neale. Saint Louis: Concordia Publishing House, 1942.

BOOKS & MEDIA

The Daughters of St. Paul operate book and media centers at the following addresses. Visit, call, or write the one nearest you today, or find us at www.pauline.org.

CALIFORNIA

3908 Sepulveda Blvd, Culver City, CA 90230	310-397-8676
935 Brewster Avenue, Redwood City, CA 94063	650-369-4230
5945 Balboa Avenue, San Diego, CA 92111	858-565-9181

FLORIDA

145 S.W. 107th Avenue, Miami, FL 33174	305-559-6715

HAWAII

1143 Bishop Street, Honolulu, HI 96813	808-521-2731

ILLINOIS

172 North Michigan Avenue, Chicago, IL 60601	312-346-4228

LOUISIANA

4403 Veterans Memorial Blvd, Metairie, LA 70006	504-887-7631

MASSACHUSETTS

885 Providence Hwy, Dedham, MA 02026	781-326-5385

MISSOURI

9804 Watson Road, St. Louis, MO 63126	314-965-3512

NEW YORK

64 W. 38th Street, New York, NY 10018	212-754-1110

SOUTH CAROLINA

243 King Street, Charleston, SC 29401	843-577-0175

TEXAS

Currently no book center; for parish exhibits or outreach evangelization, contact: 210–488–4123 or SanAntonio@paulinemedia.com

VIRGINIA

1025 King Street, Alexandria, VA 22314	703-549-3806

CANADA

3022 Dufferin Street, Toronto, ON M6B 3T5	416-781-9131

¡También somos su fuente para libros,
videos y música en español!